World Issues

GENETIC ENGINEERING

Steve Parker

Thameside Press

WORLD ISSUES

DRUGS
EQUAL OPPORTUNITIES
GENETIC ENGINEERING
POVERTY
REFUGEES

Produced by Roger Coote Publishing
Gissing's Farm, Fressingfield, Suffolk IP21 5SH, UK

Distributed in the United States by
Smart Apple Media
1980 Lookout Drive
North Mankato, MN 56003

Commissioning Editor: Jason Hook
Designer: Sarah Crouch
Consultant: Jim Mulligan, CSV
Picture Researcher: Lynda Lines

ISBN: 1-931983-28-3
Library of Congress Control Number: 2002 141374

Printed in Hong Kong/China
10 9 8 7 6 5 4 3 2 1

Picture Acknowledgements
We wish to thank the following individuals and organizations for their help and assistance, and for
supplying material in their collections: Associated Press 3 (Advanced Cell Technologies), 18 (Johns
Hopkins University), 27 (Aqua Bounty Farms), 28 (Greg Baker), 29 (Sal Veder), 31 (Chris Knight), 32
(Bob Child), 33 (Claudio Cruz), 39 (Advanced Cell Technologies), 42 (Leslie E Kossoff), 44 (Ng Han
Guan), 45 (Nati Harnik); Care International 46 (D White); Corbis 1 (Adrian Arbib), 47 (Adrian
Arbib); Corbis Stock Market 14 (Tom Stewart), 16 (LWA-Dann Tardif), 20 (Charles Gupton);
Popperfoto 7 (Reuters), 11 (Reuters), 30 (Reuters), 34 (Reuters), 35 (Reuters), 37 (Reuters), 41
(Reuters); Robert Harding Picture Library 26 (Bildagentur Schuster/Weiber), 40 (Roger Markham-
Smith); Science Photo Library front cover (J C Revy), 4 (Weiss/Jerrican), 6 (Philippe Plailly), 9
(Hugh Turvey), 10 (Simon Fraser), 12 (Dr Yorgos Nikas), 13 (Biophoto Associates), 17 (J C Revy), 19
(J C Revy), 21 (James King-Holmes), 22 (Maximillian Stock), 23 (Volkea Steger), 24 (P
Plailly/Eurelios), 25 (D Yo Trung/ Eurelios), 36 (Alex Bariel), 38 (Novosti), 43 (James King-Holmes);
Still Pictures 5 top (Max Fulcher), 5 middle (Ron Giling), 5 bottom (S Cytrynowicz). Artwork by
Michael Posen. The pictures used in this book do not show the actual people named in the case
studies in the text.

CONTENTS

Naomi's Story

Naomi works for a company in Europe that conducts scientific research into genes. She tries to find out what genes do, and how to change or "engineer" them. This is called genetic engineering, or genetic modification (GM).

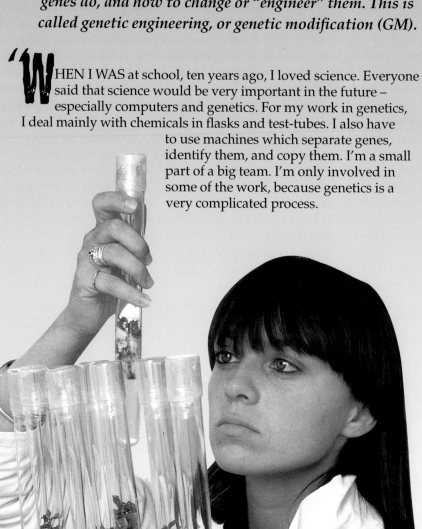

"WHEN I WAS at school, ten years ago, I loved science. Everyone said that science would be very important in the future – especially computers and genetics. For my work in genetics, I deal mainly with chemicals in flasks and test-tubes. I also have to use machines which separate genes, identify them, and copy them. I'm a small part of a big team. I'm only involved in some of the work, because genetics is a very complicated process.

To put it simply, genes are bits of chemicals inside a living thing, and they are like instructions. They tell a living thing how to grow, survive, and carry out its life processes. In our research, we find genes in one type of living thing which might be useful if we put them into another.

At the moment I am studying genes in a weed that grows in wheat fields. Sometimes insects eat the wheat, but they don't eat the weed. We're trying to find out if this is due to a certain gene in the weed. We might be able to put that gene into wheat, so that the insect can no longer damage the crop. That would save farmers money, and might even make bread cheaper.

Our research could last for years, or it might just reach a dead-end. The weed has thousands of genes, and it takes an age to study them all. When we move a gene into a different type of living thing, it might not work properly in its new 'home.' And we have to be very careful about safety. Genes are just tiny scraps of chemicals, but some people believe that if they get into the wrong place, they might create a new germ or even a dangerous mutant.

A few years ago, genetic engineering promised so much. We were going to feed the hungry, heal the sick, and save the world. Progress is happening, but it's very slow. And almost anything to do with genetics seems to cause all kinds of arguments and protests."

Genetics in three countries

Genetic engineering is not only confined to the laboratory. It can affect the food that is grown all around the world.

AUSTRALIA
Farmhouse Organics are proud that their food crops are grown "the natural way." But they are worried that pollen from GM crops on a nearby farm might be carried on the wind and affect their own crops.

EAST AFRICA
Farmers struggle yearly to grow maize in the dry soil. Some want to try a new type of maize, which they have heard is being tested in the USA. Its genes have been altered so that it can grow with less water.

SOUTH AMERICA
A local farmer has some bags of GM soy beans, as seeds to plant. He says they can be sprayed with a powerful herbicide, which will kill all weeds, allowing the crop to produce far more. Should other farmers trust him?

What Are Genes?

Imagine that you have to build a complex machine from thousands of parts. To fit them together, you need a set of instructions. A living thing is far more complicated than any machine. It has billions of parts that work together. It also needs a set of instructions so it can grow, develop, and survive. The instructions for a living thing are called genes.

THE INSTRUCTIONS FOR a machine are usually written on paper. The genes (instructions) for a living thing are in the form of a chemical substance called DNA (deoxyribonucleic acid). A machine's instructions are big enough for us to see. Genes are so tiny they can only be seen by using special microscopes. All the genes for a living thing, from a daisy or a worm to a tree or a whale, are in pieces of DNA that could fit onto the period at the end of this sentence.

What is genetic engineering?

Each living thing, such as an apple tree or a sheep, has a set of thousands of genes in the form of DNA. This DNA can be taken out by chemical methods. It looks like tiny threads of pale jelly. In genetic engineering, the DNA is split into shorter pieces. Each piece is studied to see which particular genes it contains. Then a gene can be altered, moved, removed, or put into the genes of another living thing.

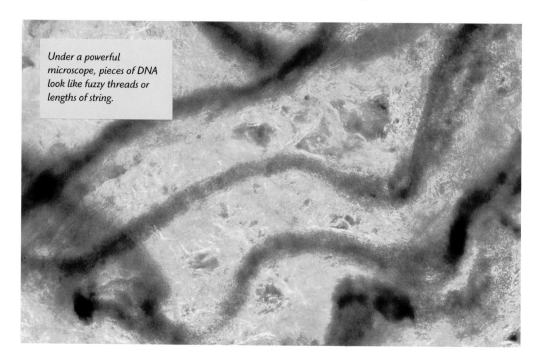

Under a powerful microscope, pieces of DNA look like fuzzy threads or lengths of string.

In June 2000, President Bill Clinton and other world leaders announced the great achievement of the Human Genome Organization (HUGO).

Is genetic engineering helpful?

Suppose that scientists study a plant that grows many large seeds. They take out and identify the genes that make the seeds big and numerous.

Then they add these genes into another type of plant, where they do not occur naturally. The genes work in their new "home," and the second plant grows more and bigger seeds. If this plant is a farm crop, this process is, of course, very helpful to the farmer. But genetics is hugely complex. Things can go wrong, and do. The rewards might be great, but there could be dangers involved that we cannot even imagine until they happen.

The Human Genome Organization

In May 2000, scientists from HUGO (Human Genome Organization) finished making the list of all the genetic material for a human being. This full set of genes is called the human genome. Bill Clinton, then president of the U.S., called it "the most wondrous map ever produced by mankind." Tony Blair, Prime Minister of Britain, said it was "a breakthrough that opens the way for massive advancement." But we still do not know exactly what each gene does, or how it works.

The shape of DNA

DNA is like a long ladder, twisted into the shape of a corkscrew. This shape is called a double-helix. It was discovered by James Watson and Francis Crick in 1953. The double-helix shape plays an important role in the way a gene is copied so that its product can be made.

How do genes work?

All living things are made of cells, which are like building blocks. Cells are so small that about 10, 000 would fit inside this *o*. There are 100 million billion in a human body. A gene of DNA is even smaller. To one gene, a cell is like a gigantic living factory.

Genes are made up of pieces of DNA. Each piece of DNA is made up of smaller pieces or sub-units called bases, which

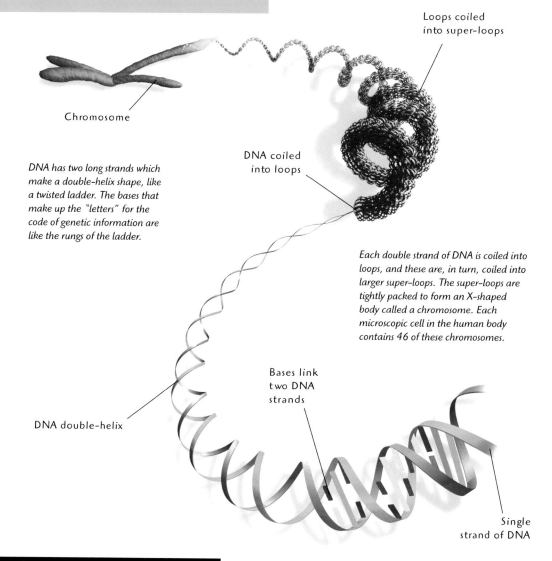

Loops coiled into super-loops

Chromosome

DNA has two long strands which make a double-helix shape, like a twisted ladder. The bases that make up the "letters" for the code of genetic information are like the rungs of the ladder.

DNA coiled into loops

Each double strand of DNA is coiled into loops, and these are, in turn, coiled into larger super-loops. The super-loops are tightly packed to form an X-shaped body called a chromosome. Each microscopic cell in the human body contains 46 of these chromosomes.

DNA double-helix

Bases link two DNA strands

Single strand of DNA

are joined together in a long row like beads on a necklace. In the same way that a word carries information by the order of its letters, a gene carries information by the order of its bases. We use 26 different letters to make words. DNA has only four different bases. But each gene has hundreds or thousands of them, so it can carry a huge amount of information. The whole set of human genes has 3,100 million pairs of bases.

What is RNA?

For a gene to work, the order of its bases is copied into another substance very similar to DNA, called RNA (ribonucleic acid). The RNA then goes to another place inside the cell, where it carries out its job – almost like a person in a factory. It gathers together various substances or raw materials and fixes them together in the right order, following the instructions in the original gene.

What do genes make?

The result of this process is a product – a substance, or protein, in the body. An example is the substance that gives the eyes their color. In one person, the product is blue, so the eyes are blue. We say that the person has the gene for blue eyes. In another person the gene for eye color has a slightly different order of bases. This gives a brown product for brown eyes.

A whole human body needs between 30, 000 and 40, 000 different types of gene. Every tiny cell contains all of these genes. But in any single cell, only some of the genes are "switched on." The rest are "switched off." In the cells at the front of the eye, the genes for eye color are "on" and make their product. Other genes are "off" and make nothing. The fact that all the cells contain all the types of gene is very important in genetic engineering.

Eye color is determined by a certain gene. The different versions of the gene give eyes of different colors.

How are genes "engineered?"

Genes can be separated, studied, and joined back together. This can be done by manipulating DNA, the chemical that makes up genes.

To obtain genes, you need just a tiny piece of a living thing, such as a strand of hair, a flake of skin, or a flower petal. Even such a tiny piece contains millions of cells, and every cell contains the full set of the living thing's genes.

The first step to identifying genes is to heat the cells with chemicals to make them release their contents. These are then spun around very fast in a centrifuge machine (like a spin dryer), which separates them into different layers. The DNA layer is thin and pale, and looks like damp cotton. Its threads can be wound onto a glass rod.

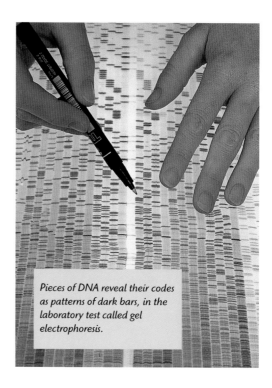

Pieces of DNA reveal their codes as patterns of dark bars, in the laboratory test called gel electrophoresis.

DEBATE - Is genetic engineering an art form?

When blue light shines on Alba the rabbit, she glows green. The reason for this is that Alba was given a gene from a jellyfish. This gene makes the jellyfish glow naturally in the dark ocean. Alba was created as "living art" for Eduardo Kac, in Chicago. She seems healthy and happy, but is this type of genetic engineering acceptable?

- Yes. Alba is a work of art, and should be admired.
- No. People should not alter genes for the sake of art. It should be done only for serious reasons, such as healing people or growing more food.

The long lengths of DNA are split into shorter ones by warming them with various chemicals called REs (restriction enzymes). These short fragments of DNA are identified by adding them to yet more chemicals, putting them in a clear gel, and passing electricity through the gel. This makes different fragments move different distances along the gel. Called gel electrophoresis, this process creates a row of lines that look like a supermarket bar-code. This identifies the DNA piece, and so identifies the gene.

How are genes put into new living things?

The fragments of DNA are genes or parts of genes. They can be added to the genes of another living thing by using microscopic life-forms called phages to "carry" them. The phages, which are a type of virus, are put in a flask with copies of the new gene. Some of them take the new gene into themselves. The phages are then added to other cells, such as the cells of an animal.

These fish have been genetically altered by adding a gene from another animal. The gene makes a substance that glows in the dark. The fish are both GMOs and unusual pets.

What is a GMO?

Phages are so small that they can get into a cell and add the new gene to it. The altered cell is then encouraged to divide and make more cells like itself. As it divides and makes more cells, it can even be made to develop into a whole living thing. This new living thing is called a transgenic life-form or GMO (genetically modified organism).

What Are Genetic Conditions?

Every human body starts as a tiny egg cell inside its mother's womb. This egg cell contains all the genes it needs to grow and develop into a newborn baby and then a full-grown human. But in a few cases, there is a fault in the genes. The result may be a genetic condition, which affects health and normal life. About 1 or 2 babies in every 100 are born with a genetic condition.

THE GENES FOR the human body are instructions, not only for the finished body, but for the developing and growing process, too. If there is a tiny fault, such as a missing gene or one which is slightly altered, the body may not be able to develop or work normally.

A highly magnified view of the egg cell from which a new human body will grow.

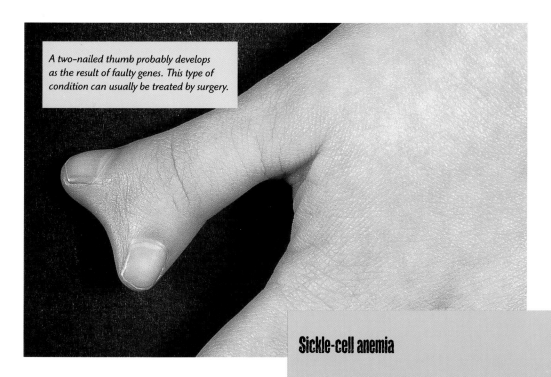

A two-nailed thumb probably develops as the result of faulty genes. This type of condition can usually be treated by surgery.

There are thousands of different genetic conditions. Some have little effect on health, although they may be noticeable. Examples are a red mark on the skin, called a birthmark, or an extra finger or toe. Other genetic conditions can cause serious health problems. If the heart does not develop in the normal way, for example, it may not pump blood around the body effectively.

Why do genes become faulty?

At the start of development, the single egg cell splits into two cells. Then each of these cells also divides into two, and so on. The total number of cells becomes 4, 8, 16, 32, and gradually increases to hundreds, thousands, and millions to build the growing body.

Every time a cell divides, its full set of genes is copied. This happens because the lengths of DNA, which form the genes, make exact copies of themselves. So, the two cells from every division each have a full set of genes.

Sickle-cell anemia

Some genetic conditions are not obvious from the outside, but they can greatly affect the way the body works. We breathe in and out to get oxygen from the air, and the oxygen is carried around the body by our blood. In a genetic condition called sickle-cell anemia, the blood cannot carry this oxygen properly. This can result in severe illness or death.

Very rarely, this copying process goes wrong. A gene can get altered, missed out, or put into the wrong place in the whole set. This change is called a "mutation." Often, the reasons for this are unknown. In other cases, there is a known cause that interferes with gene copying. Causes can include germs, harmful drugs, and chemicals, and dangerous rays such as radioactivity.

Each child receives a unique set of genes from its two parents (apart from identical twins, which have the same genes).

How are genetic conditions passed on?

A human body can develop a genetic condition as it grows in the mother's womb, after birth, or even later in life. But in some cases the condition is there at the beginning, in the tiny, fertilized egg cell. It has been passed on from one or both parents. This is known as an "inherited condition," and it can happen in various ways.

The fertilized egg cell contains two sets of human genes. One set came from the mother, who produced the egg cell. The other set came from the father, who produced the sperm cell. During fertilization, the sperm cell joins with the egg cell. Because the fertilized egg

cell has two full sets of genes, every cell in the resulting body has them, too. In other words, the genes occur in pairs.

Sometimes one gene in a pair is faulty, but the other one is normal. In certain cases, the normal gene is allowed to work in the usual way, because the faulty gene (known as a recessive gene) "gives in." In other cases, the faulty gene of a pair does not "give in." In fact it "takes over." It does not allow the normal gene to work properly, and so a problem results. This type of faulty gene is known as a "dominant gene." It can cause conditions such as tuberous sclerosis, which affects the skin and brain.

On very rare occasions, both parents may pass the faulty version of a gene to their baby. So, the baby receives a pair of genes, one from each parent, and both are faulty. In this case, there is no normal version to make the faulty gene "give in." This can create conditions such as sickle-cell anemia.

There are more than 1,500 different medical conditions caused by a fault in a single gene inherited from a parent. There are thousands more that are caused not by one faulty gene, but by two or more. These are described as "multiple-gene conditions."

This diagram shows how cystic fibrosis can be inherited. In each parent, one of the pair of genes is normal and the other is faulty. It depends on chance which two genes pass to the offspring, giving four possible combinations.

In the family

It is known that genes play a part in many conditions and illnesses. But it is not always clear how many genes are involved, or exactly how they cause the problem. It is simply too complicated to work out. Examples are the breathing problems of asthma, the skin disorders of eczema, various allergies, and certain types of heart disease. We say that the condition "runs in the family." Doctors might say there is "an inherited tendency" or "a genetic component."

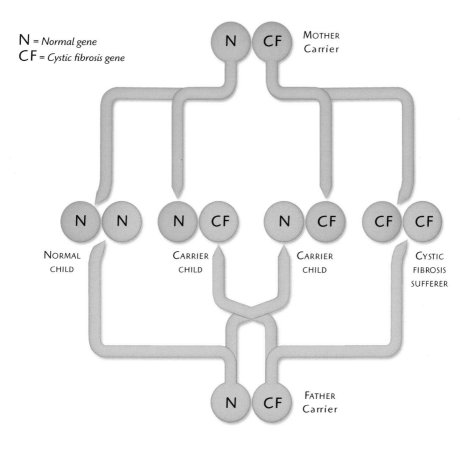

N = *Normal gene*
CF = *Cystic fibrosis gene*

MOTHER
Carrier

NORMAL CHILD

CARRIER CHILD

CARRIER CHILD

CYSTIC FIBROSIS SUFFERER

FATHER
Carrier

Can genetic conditions be predicted?

Genetic conditions vary greatly, in the ways that they are passed from parent to child, and in their effects on health and well being. And there are many ways to predict them, detect them if they occur, and stop or treat them.

Sometimes, genetic conditions can be predicted by experts called genetic counselors. If an inherited condition has occurred in the parents' families, the genetic counselor may be able to figure out the chances that their baby will have it, too. This may be stated in a fairly accurate way, such as a "3-in-4" risk. If only one parent has the condition, or it has occurred only in relatives such as brothers or aunts, the risk may be less.

Sometimes a counselor advises parents to have tests on their blood or other body parts. As we have seen, genes occur in pairs, and it is possible that one gene of the pair is faulty, but the other is normal. Without undergoing tests, the parent might not be aware that he or she "carries" a faulty gene that might be passed on to the baby.

Can genetic conditions be treated?

Some genetic conditions can be detected and even treated when the baby is still in the womb. Others can be treated soon after birth, by a surgical operation or

The genetic counselor is a medically trained doctor who specializes in how conditions are inherited.

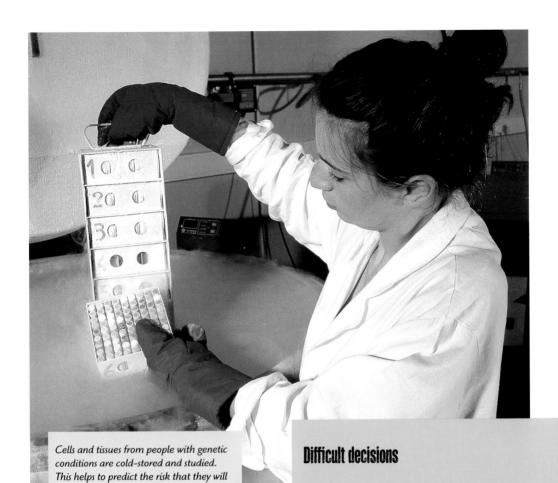

Cells and tissues from people with genetic conditions are cold-stored and studied. This helps to predict the risk that they will pass the condition to their own children.

medicinal drugs. The long-term outlook for the baby could be a normal life. But certain conditions have more serious long-term results. These can affect not only the health of the baby as it grows up, but also schooling and many aspects of family life.

The parents-to-be need to discuss the risks and outlook. Their desire to have a baby may be so strong that they decide to take a risk. Or they may consider other options. These can include staying "child-free," adopting a baby, or using sperm or eggs donated from somebody without the faulty gene.

Difficult decisions

Some serious genetic conditions can be detected while the baby is still very tiny, in the womb. An example is spina bifida, where the nerves of the spinal cord and brain do not form properly. If this is detected, parents might consider termination of pregnancy (also known as abortion). Views on this vary. Some countries offer it as part of the medical system, while others forbid it by law. Some religions or faiths forbid it. Termination can be seen as murder, or as a way of saving a child and its family from pain and suffering.

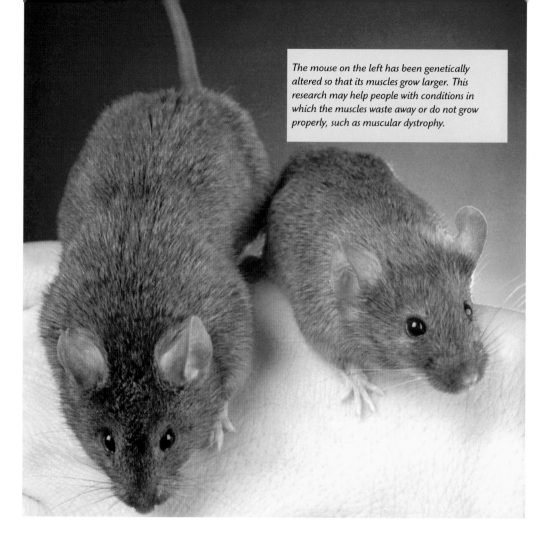

The mouse on the left has been genetically altered so that its muscles grow larger. This research may help people with conditions in which the muscles waste away or do not grow properly, such as muscular dystrophy.

What is gene therapy?

A person's genes are inside every microscopic cell of their body. If there is a genetic fault in the initial egg cell, then every cell will have the same fault in its genes. Scientists are working on correcting these faults with new forms of treatment called "gene therapy."

In almost every body part, millions of tiny new cells are made every day to replace those that wear out and die. In a genetic condition, all of these cells have the fault. In gene therapy, the aim is to correct the fault by replacing the affected genes with normal ones, or to put in new cells that do not contain the faulty genes.

Can gene therapy treat cystic fibrosis?

Cystic fibrosis (see *page 15*) affects about 1 child in every 2,000. The gene that causes it has been identified. It contains the instructions to make the natural slimy mucus that protects the insides of the lungs. But the faulty gene makes the mucus much thicker than normal. The lungs get clogged, and the person suffers coughs, infections, and many other problems.

Gene therapy aims to add the normal mucus-making genes to cells in the lungs, by "carriers" such as genetically engineered viruses. But this is proving difficult. Some lung cells take up the new genes and use them for a time.

But gradually these altered cells wear out and die. They are replaced by cells with the faulty gene, and the problem comes back.

What are stem cells?

One way around this difficulty is to carry out treatment before birth, when many cells of the body have not yet become specialized to do particular jobs. These unspecialized cells are called "stem cells." They are more likely to take up altered genes in a permanent way and allow the genes to work. Then the genes can pass to all the cells that develop from the stem cells. In the case of cystic fibrosis, normal mucus-making genes might continue to pass to lung cells for years or even a lifetime.

However, this type of treatment means testing a very tiny baby in the womb to see if it has the condition. This brings

The site of the faulty gene that causes cystic fibrosis is arrowed in red, on the full set of human chromosomes.

its own risks and problems. Work on cystic fibrosis and many other genetic conditions has been slow, and some results have been disappointing.

DEBATE – Should gene therapy be allowed?

If gene therapy becomes possible, it could involve testing tiny babies before birth, or even screening single egg cells for genetic problems. Should this be allowed?

* No. Gene therapy is not natural. Who would have the power to choose which conditions to detect, and whether the egg or tiny baby should continue development?

* Yes. Any therapy that means more babies are born healthy must be a good thing.

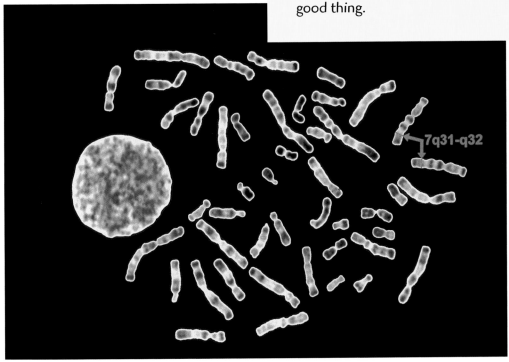

7q31-q32

What Is Biotechnology?

Biotechnology is both a science and an industry.
It combines biology, which is the science of living things,
with technology, the science of industry and machines.

IN A SIMPLE form, biotechnology goes back hundreds of years. For example, bread is made using tiny living things called yeasts. As bread dough is baked in an oven, the yeasts in it make a gas called carbon dioxide. This produces tiny bubbles that make the bread "rise" and develop its distinctive spongy texture.

Another example of traditional biotechnology is the fermenting of beer and wine. Yeasts are again used, and they work as tiny "living factories." The yeast cells make thousands or millions of identical products, just like a factory, but the products are made by living processes, not mechanical ones. The yeast cells naturally produce

Patenting life

"The biotech industry was spawned when the US Supreme Court ruled in 1980 that it was legal to patent genetically created life."

Source: Scientific American magazine, July 2000, in its special industry report "The Business of the Human Genome."

Processes such as baking bread, brewing wine and growing yoghurt involve living things and so are part-biological.

Quicker copies

Every time a microscopic cell splits or divides, the DNA of its genes is copied, so that each of the two resulting cells receives a full set of genes. This process can be used to produce extra copies of DNA for genetic engineering. But this "cell-growth" method is slow, and sometimes the cells die or the DNA gets altered. In the late 1980s, a new method was developed called PCR (polymerase chain reaction). This chemical technique is much faster and more reliable than cell growth. It can make a million copies of a gene, as lengths of DNA, in a couple of hours. PCR is now a vital part of genetic research.

alcohol as a waste substance, which is the most important ingredient of beer and wine.

Over hundreds of years, when making bread, beer, and wine, people have chosen which kinds of yeast to use. If a new type of yeast appeared naturally, and it gave tastier bread or better-flavored wine, people saved this yeast and used it again. Sometimes yeasts were mixed together to try to combine the best features of each, by combining their genes. This method of choosing or selecting from what is available in nature is called "selective breeding," or artificial selection. But it takes a long time and depends greatly on chance.

What is GE biotech?

GE biotech (genetically engineered biotechnology) does not simply use natural types of yeast, bacteria, and other microbes as "living factories." Instead, scientists modify or engineer the genes of these microbes, usually by adding a specific gene from another living thing. This can be done quickly and accurately. Then the microbes produce not only their own useful substances, but also substances that we might find useful.

Growth hormone

The body's growth is controlled by a natural chemical substance called growth hormone. Some people do not have enough growth hormone and grow very slowly. They can be given extra growth hormone by injection. Previously, the hormone was obtained from dead bodies and was extremely costly. Genetically engineered bacteria now make growth hormone in larger amounts for less cost. This means many more affected people can receive treatment and grow normally.

How does GE biotech work?

The basics of GE biotech are similar to those of many other genetic methods. A living thing that has a useful product is studied to identify the gene for making that product. This gene is then separated or isolated, as one or more pieces of DNA. These are added, or "spliced" into another life-form, which will act as a "living factory" and produce the useful product.

What is *E. coli*?

One of the main living things used in GE biotech is a type of bacterium called *E. coli* (*Escherischia coli*). This is a single-celled, rod-shaped life-form about one-hundredth of one millimeter long. *E. coli* can be grown quickly and easily in a warm "soup" of nutrients, in a large flask or vat. Billions of genetically engineered *E. coli* in the vat divide every 20 to 30 minutes, to keep up their

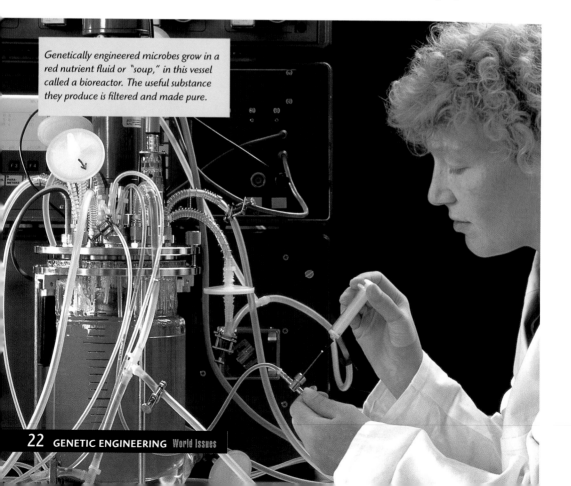

Genetically engineered microbes grow in a red nutrient fluid or "soup," in this vessel called a bioreactor. The useful substance they produce is filtered and made pure.

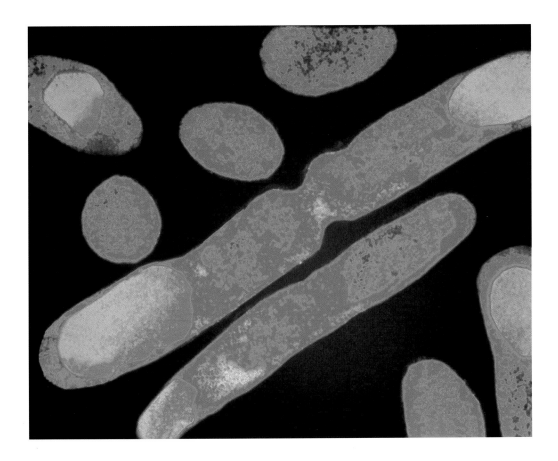

numbers as old ones die. When a new gene is added to them, the *E. coli* make the product the gene tells them to. The product is then filtered, or tapped, from the vat and purified for use.

These E. coli *bacteria have been genetically altered to make the human hormone, insulin, in their orange areas. They are shown about 20, 000 times larger than life.*

What important products are made?

One of GE biotech's early successes was the production of insulin. This is an important natural chemical in the body, called a hormone. It controls the way the body uses its main energy source, sugar. People who lack insulin suffer from the condition called diabetes. They can become very ill or even die.

The normal treatment is to replace the missing insulin with regular injections. Insulin for these injections used to be obtained from farm animals. However, their forms of insulin are slightly different from the human type of insulin. In the 1980s, the gene for making human insulin was identified and put into *E. coli* bacteria. These bacteria can use the gene as their "instructions" and make human insulin for injection.

GE biotech has also been used to produce clotting factor, which can be given to people with the genetic condition called hemophilia, so that their blood clots normally. By using this clotting factor, hemophiliacs avoid the need for transfusions, which carry the risk of infections from contaminated blood, such as AIDS and hepatitis.

What else can GE biotech produce?

In the past few years, there has been a huge amount of research into how new products could be made by living things that have been genetically engineered. Not only bacteria and similar microbes, but whole plants and animals could be used as "living factories."

Some of the most important GE biotech products are medicinal drugs. Microbes have been genetically engineered to make antibiotic drugs that kill germs and stop infectious diseases. They can also produce the drug interferon, which treats some diseases caused by viruses and fights certain types of cancer.

Mussel power

Shellfish called mussels stick firmly to rocks, and one hope in biotechnology is that genetically engineered versions might be gathered and processed to create new kinds of superglue.

Oilseed rape plants are tested to see if they have taken up a new gene. It tells them to produce a substance vital in the human body, which is lacking in some people with genetic conditions.

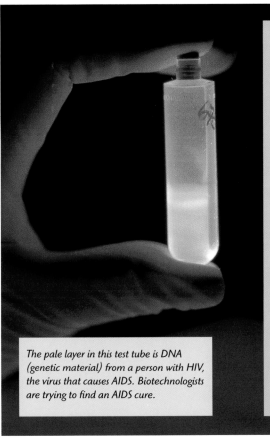

The pale layer in this test tube is DNA (genetic material) from a person with HIV, the virus that causes AIDS. Biotechnologists are trying to find an AIDS cure.

The biotech banana

One of the main plant foods for genetic research is the banana. It might be possible to engineer bananas to contain the vaccines that immunize, or protect, us against diseases. There would be no need for injections – simply eat a genetically engineered banana. The banana has been chosen because it is widely available, and it comes "packed" in its skin so it is clean and hygienic when eaten. Also, most children and adults like bananas. A less popular choice would be the genetically engineered cabbage!

Some of the vaccines given to babies and children, to give them lifelong protection against diseases, are also GE biotech products.

How can plants and animals be used?

Another area of research is concerned with putting the genes for a medicinal drug, vaccine, or other useful product into a plant grown as food. In this way, people could receive their treatment by eating the food. However, if the genetically engineered food looks the same as the natural food, people who do not need the treatment might eat it, too, by mistake.

Research has also shown that farm animals such as sheep and goats can be given the genes to make medicinal

drugs or similar products. The useful product is obtained from their milk. An example is the drug antithrombin, which stops blood from clotting too much.

Plants such as oilseed rape and sunflowers are grown for their oil. Genetically engineered forms of these plants might produce oil that can be used in specially adapted vehicle engines. This could help to reduce air pollution and save normal oil and gas resources.

Genetically engineered bacteria might also be capable of helping to break down sewage and similar wastes faster than naturally occurring bacteria. This might lessen the problems of waste disposal and sewage pollution.

Does Genetic Engineering Affect My Food?

Farming is one of the main areas in which genetic engineering can be used. Scientists are studying the genes of hundreds of species of plant and animal which are farmed to provide food for people.

ALTERING CROPS AND farm animals by modifying their genes is nothing new. People have been doing it for thousands of years. Wheat, barley, rice, potatoes, oranges, and other farm plants, as well as cows, sheep, goats, chickens, and other farm animals, have all been bred from wild ancestors.

What is selective breeding?

Long ago, people began to gather naturally growing plants such as wild wheat, and use them as food. Some wild wheat plants grew bigger grains than others, and people tended to choose the plants with bigger grains for the next year's crop. This happened many times,

and gradually the grains became larger and larger, creating domesticated, or farmed, wheat. If another type of wheat was found with a useful feature, like a stronger stalk, this was also used by breeding the two types together. This whole process is called selective breeding (see *page 21*).

Farm animals were also produced by selective breeding. Cows that gave the most milk were allowed to have calves, with the aim that female calves would receive their mother's genes for producing lots of milk. Gradually, by selecting individual cows for their "high-milk" genes, milk yields increased.

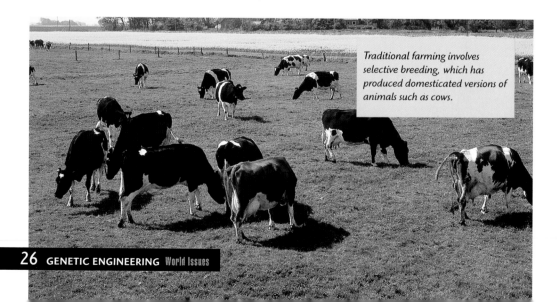

Traditional farming involves selective breeding, which has produced domesticated versions of animals such as cows.

These two salmon are the same age. But the genetically engineered one has grown almost twice as fast as normal.

Super salmon

Genetic engineering has created "super salmon" that have a gene for faster growth. In fact, they grow up to six times faster than normal salmon. In future they could be farmed in large pools or in giant cages suspended in the sea, as normal salmon are today.

How is genetic engineering different?

Selective breeding needs many generations of parents and offspring. It takes many years, even centuries, to produce results. Genetic engineering, on the other hand, is very fast. Altering the genes in a laboratory can be done in a few weeks, or even days, and all within one generation.

Traditional selective breeding uses the natural mating process of two individuals of the same species. So, genes can only be altered within the same species of living thing. For example, cows cannot breed with sheep. This of course means that a sheep's genes for growing a thick, wooly coat could not be transferred to a cow. But in genetic engineering, in theory, genes can be moved from one species of living thing to almost any other. So a cow could receive a gene from a sheep. It could also receive genes from a whale, or an insect, or even a holly bush or a mushroom. But the important and difficult question is whether the gene would work in its new "home."

This Chinese merchant sells corn and soya seeds that are genetically engineered to resist disease.

Golden rice

Rice is the main food for more than half the world's people. A GM variety called "golden rice" is designed to provide the body with more vitamin A. Lack of vitamin A is thought to kill up to 2 million people each year around the world. Golden rice could prevent many of these deaths. Tests on growing the rice, called field trials, are due to begin around 2005.

Why genetically engineer crops?

Genetic engineering can create crops that are resistant to weedkiller sprays, so the sprays can be used to kill weeds without harming the crop. It can allow crops to produce a substance that will deter insects from eating them.
It can make crops resistant to diseases caused by microbes known as viruses. Genetic engineering can also improve the quality and quantity of crops, giving them the advantages of faster growth, bigger yields, and better flavor.

Genetic engineering might also allow plants to grow in a wider range of growing conditions. If genetically engineered wheat could grow in drier soil, or survive a short drought, it might grow in places where normal wheat cannot survive, and so produce food in areas of famine.

What else is possible?

Certain genes can control ripening, so all of a crop is ready to harvest on the same day. Other genes can make soft fruits less prone to damage, marks, and bruises as they are picked, packed, transported, and put on display.

The appearance of a food plant can also be changed, so that apples look shiny and smooth rather than dull and wrinkled. It might even be possible to change the colors of plants and animals by genetic engineering and create "novelty" foods such as blue tomatoes or red peas!

How widespread are GM crops?

In the year 2000, GM crops were grown worldwide in an area about twice the size of Oregon. That is an area 20 times bigger than in 1995. More than three-quarters of GM crops grown worldwide are varieties of soya and maize. However, by no means all GM crops are being grown by ordinary farmers in ordinary fields, as food for people. Some are still being researched. Others are being test-grown in greenhouses or in "field trials" on small, carefully controlled plots of land.

Savor the flavor

One of the first genetically engineered foods to go on sale to the public was the Flavr-Savr tomato. It was introduced into 730 stores in the USA in late 1994. It had been engineered to stay fresh on the shelf for a long time, holding its flavor well instead of becoming squishy and rotten. But opposition from farmers and consumers, along with problems growing the tomatoes on a large scale, eventually led to the Flavr-Savr being withdrawn from the market.

Early research on GM tomatoes showed promise. But several types of problems combined to prevent widespread success.

Can GM foods harm me?

In theory, it is possible that new genes put into food plants and animals could damage the human body. As yet, there is no firm evidence that this has ever happened. But that does not mean that it never will.

Genes added to a food product, such as a farm crop, are intended to have certain effects – but they might also have other, unexpected effects. They could cause the plant to produce extra amounts of its natural chemicals. In normal amounts these cause no problems, but larger amounts might be poisonous. Or the new genes might make the plant produce entirely new, unexpected substances, which could be toxic or cause allergies.

Could food genes get into the body?

New genes in food, as pieces of DNA, might somehow "escape" into the body of the person eating it, through the lining of the stomach and gut. The genes might even attach themselves to human genes, with yet more unknown results. Over many years, could GM foods trigger complex diseases such as cancer? Or reduce the body's resistance to germs and infection? Or even have gradual effects on intelligence?

Supporters of genetic engineering argue that millions of people have been eating GM foods for several years, and there are no proven cases of harm being caused. Also, GM foods undergo extremely extensive tests and trials. These are conducted in the laboratory,

In February 2000, masked protesters demonstrate outside a conference on GM foods. Campaigners insist that the long-term effects of such foods are not known and may never be clear.

Tobacco can be altered genetically in various ways. This version aims to contain less of the drug nicotine, so that smoking it causes less harm than normal tobacco.

on animals, and on people acting as volunteers. Indeed, GM foods are tested far more than those made by traditional methods of selective breeding.

Am I eating GM food?

It can be relatively simple to identify "single" GM food products such as GM potatoes, oranges, or chickens. Many producers and supermarkets already label them, so the consumer can choose whether to eat them. But foodstuffs such as maize and soya are bought, sold, mixed, and blended several times, and used as ingredients in sauces, gravies, pies, fillings, pizzas, and ready-cooked meals. It is not always easy, or even possible, to know if a processed or ready-cooked item contains GM foodstuffs. Arranging a system to label these products might be possible, but so complex and expensive that it would increase the price of food.

DEBATE - Should genetic engineering be used on tobacco?

Genetic engineering is being carried out to improve tobacco production. Do you think that money should be spent on this?

- Yes. Tobacco is a valuable crop. Its industry employs millions and brings money to poor regions. It is therefore important to study genetic engineering for tobacco.

- No. Smoking tobacco causes massive amounts of illness, suffering, and death. The money spent on GM tobacco should be put towards more important and healthier aims, such as developing GM rice.

GM maize is studied carefully in the contained, controlled surroundings of a glasshouse. This helps to reduce the risks of genes escaping into the environment.

DEBATE - Should GM crop trials be stopped?

- No. Studies under secure, contained conditions will allow scientists to gather important information. Growing GM plants alongside their "normal" domesticated version in a greenhouse would show if genes might "jump" into them.
- Yes. All GM trials are dangerous. The history of science shows that no amount of testing can ever detect every possible problem.

Will GM farming damage the environment?

As we farm plants and animals for food, and GM crops are introduced, it might turn out to be impossible to keep the "GMs" away from the "normals." A GM individual might then interbreed with a non-GM one. Gradually, the new gene might "escape" into the wild and spread into the natural population. The effects are certainly unpredictable, and they could be disastrous.

At first, a new GM plant such as GM wheat is grown in a laboratory and then in larger numbers in a greenhouse. Plants are carefully studied to see if their growth is healthy and whether they produce any unusual new substances. Their useful parts, such as the grains in wheat, are tested for ill-effects by feeding them to animals. After the initial tests and studies have been completed, the GM crop is grown in small batches in "field trials."

How might genes escape?

In most crops, the male parts of a flower release thousands of tiny pollen grains. They blow on the wind or are carried by creatures such as bees or birds to the female parts of a flower of the same kind. A male cell in the pollen grain joins with a female cell in the flower to start the development of a new seed.

It is possible that male pollen grains from a GM plant could reach the female parts of a non-GM plant of the same kind, in another field. The new genes might get into the seeds of that plant, and then be spread again by the pollen. In this way the new gene could spread long distances, perhaps even across continents. The new gene might spread to the original wild version of the plant and change nature forever.

Precautions are taken to stop this from happening. Field trials of GM crops have to be carried out a certain distance from any non-GM fields of that crop. But studies show that some pollen grains can blow on the wind for at least 30 miles. And birds and bees can spread seeds and pollen even farther afield.

Spending the money

"If the same money and effort were spent on natural farming and organic foods, as big business spends on genetically engineered crops – we would not need genetic engineering at all."

Source: International News on Genetic Engineering in Agriculture, *1999*

Domesticated, rather than wild, forms of corn have spread to almost all areas of Mexico. Will new varieties of GM corn spread the same way, despite efforts to restrict them?

What effects could escaped genes have?

The possibility that a gene might transfer from a properly tested GM plant or animal into natural populations of plants and animals is exceedingly small. But the possible results, if this did occur, are almost endless. In a laboratory or glasshouse, there is an excellent chance of restricting the spread of a gene. But in the outside world, little can be done to halt it or get it back.

Suppose that a GM crop plant has a gene to resist a certain weedkiller spray. Out in the field, the crop suffers from a disease caused by a virus. Some of the viruses take up the gene. Then they infect a weed nearby, and pass the gene on to it. The weed might then become a "superweed," resistant to the weedkiller, and spread to cause huge damage. This is entirely possible. The exact same process of "carrier" viruses transferring genes from one type of living thing to another is used in genetic engineering itself.

Imagine another case. A "superpig" gene causes baby pigs to grow much bigger and faster. One day, one escapes and breeds with its natural cousin, the wild boar. The gene is passed, stage by stage, into the local wild boar population. This creates a new breed of "superboar" that wreaks havoc on the environment.

Some oilseed rape plants grown in Britain in 2000 were genetically altered – yet the farmers did not know. Have the new genes already spread into the surroundings?

Campaigners disrupt GM corn (maize) field trails in Germany. Once campaigners have done some damage, the results of the trials are spoiled and cannot be used as truly scientific proof.

Can genes be "put back?"

Genetic engineering supporters argue that the chances of genes escaping, jumping to other living things, and then actually working in them, are so small as to be almost zero. But opponents compare the risk to the myth of the genie in the bottle. The genie promises to grant wishes, but the person who makes the wish does not think of all the possible consequences.

Anti-GM supporters say that once a new gene has escaped into nature, it can never be recaptured. Superweeds might smother the land, superbugs spread plagues, and superanimals endanger lives. You cannot put the genie, or the gene, back in the bottle.

Anti-GM campaigns

In 1999 at several sites in Britain, anti–GM campaigners disrupted field trials of GM maize, chopping down and burning the plants. The field trials were legal and were following testing guidelines. But the protesters said the trials had been hushed up, and the dangers of the trials had not been resolved. In court, no protesters were found guilty of any offense.

What Is Cloning?

Clones are living things that have exactly the same genes as each other. Cloning involves manipulating or moving sets of genes. It does not necessarily involve genetic engineering techniques such as adding or taking away individual genes. But the techniques of cloning are used in genetic engineering and vice-versa.

CLONING HAPPENS IN nature when identical twins are born. They come from the same egg cell, so they have exactly the same genes. Cloning has also been used for centuries by gardeners. They take a plant cutting, such as a piece of stem, and grow it into a whole new plant. This plant has exactly the same genes as its parent – it is a clone.

How are clones made?

Every microscopic cell in a living thing has the full set of genes. It should be possible to take this full set out of its cell, as lengths of DNA, and put it into an egg cell that has had its own DNA removed. Inside this new "home," conditions are suited to all genes being "switched on." So, they become the instructions for the whole living thing.

Identical twins have the same genes as each other. However, they develop their own individual personalities, likes and dislikes. They are not identical people.

Dolly was the first mammal cloned from the cell of an adult (rather than an embryo).

Until the mid-1990s, this could only be done with DNA removed from cells at a very early stage of development – embryo cells from the growing ball that is formed when a fertilized egg splits to form new cells. When cloning cells at such an early stage of their development, it is not possible to predict the exact type of adults that will be produced. For example, when cloning the embryo cells from a sheep, the hope might be that the cloned sheep will all have extra-quality wool. But this cannot be known for sure until the cloned sheep grow up into adults.

Can adult cells be cloned?

The answer to this problem is to clone body cells from an adult living thing, rather than embryo cells. But this raises a different problem. In a body cell from an adult, unlike a cell from an embryo, many of the genes are "switched off." Only a few are "on," because the cell is doing a specialized job in the adult body.

Hello, Dolly

Dolly the sheep was born in July 1996 in Edinburgh, Scotland. She was not the first clone of an animal. But she was the first mammal to be cloned from a specialized cell, taken from an adult. Dolly showed that in principle any cell from any living thing, even an adult, could be used to make a clone.

However, in the mid-1990s, ways were developed to "switch on" genes in a specialized adult cell, by various methods. These methods include applying chemicals, heat, and electric currents to the cells as they grow in a flask or dish in the laboratory. Dolly the sheep was the first mammal to be produced this way.

These rabbits are, in effect, identical twins. But they were born to different mothers – they are clones. The aim of cloning is to produce exact genetic copies, so the animals themselves vary as little as possible.

DEBATE - Should animals and plants be cloned?

- Yes. Genetically engineered animals could make very useful products, such as medicinal drugs. This ability can be lost in normal breeding methods, which cause genetic variety. Cloning can keep the ability, without the "waste" from natural breeding.
- No. Cloning techniques also involve "waste" – such as the many embryos lost in the Dolly experiments. Herds of cloned animals might also be wiped out through disease.

What benefits could cloning have?

Clones of useful plants have been made for centuries. Today, many types of fruit, such as bananas and strawberries, are grown by cloning. Since the birth of Dolly the sheep, many clones of animals have also been made by scientists. They range from frogs and mice to pigs and cows. Could a combination of genetic engineering and cloning help our future world? What are the costs and the risks?

To create Dolly, more than 270 attempts were made. They involved obtaining single cells from adult sheep, taking the genes out or activating them, and putting them into the wombs of female sheep, so that they behaved as egg cells and developed into newborn lambs. The losses represented many dead embryos and disrupted pregnancies.

There are many possible benefits of cloning. A champion egg-laying hen or milk-yielding cow might be cloned to give thousands of offspring with the same genes. When these animals are produced by normal breeding methods, genetic variety occurs – some offspring are not quite so successful at their required task, and production is lower. But with cloning, the animal's genes are copied exactly.

Are there drawbacks to cloning?

Cloning does have drawbacks. In normal breeding, the variety in genes gives each individual a different resistance to disease. If a disease strikes a normally bred flock or herd on a farm, some animals may die, but others might recover. If the herd or flock were clones, the disease could wipe them all out, since they have no genetic variety to protect them. The same applies to plants.

Natural breeding also sometimes produces a new and useful feature – such as bigger grains in a wheat plant – by a chance change or "mutation" in the DNA. This is part of the idea of biodiversity – having a large, varied, and naturally changing collection of genes in a whole population of living things. If animals were made by cloning, new changes and combinations could not occur.

These five cows are clones, created by scientists working in biotechnology companies in the United States.

Should humans be cloned?

The technology exists to make human clones and to genetically engineer human cells. Cloned human embryos have already been produced. Should this work continue, or are the consequences too dangerous?

Would human clones grow up to look and behave exactly the same as each other? Then a top soldier might be cloned to produce a world-dominating army. In fact, clones would not all behave the same. Identical twins are clones. They look similar, but they have individual experiences and develop their own personalities. Even though they have the same genes, identical twins end up different.

What uses could human cloning have?

If a person develops a disease in one body part, cells might be taken out from another body part to help. In the laboratory, various genes in these cells could be switched on or off to make healthy new cells. These cloned cells could be grown into a new body part to replace the diseased one. Cells for this task could also have been taken from a person while they were still an embryo in the womb. These stem cells are easier to alter and manipulate than cells that are taken from an adult body.

Cloning of cells for the treatment of illness, rather than the growing of new human beings, is called "therapeutic cloning." It could solve the problem of rejection in transplants. When a body part such as a kidney is transplanted from one person to another, the receiving body fights against this "foreign" part and tries to destroy it. This should not happen with therapeutic cloning.

Soldiers in uniform look almost identical outside, like clones. Clones are identical "inside," in their genes. But they would still be affected differently by their individual experiences and environments.

Jose Cibelli, of Advanced Cell Technology in Worcester, Massachusetts, which announced the first cloning of a human embryo.

DEBATE - Should pigs be used as living spare-part stores?

A pig could be genetically altered so that if its parts are put into a human body, they are not rejected. The pig could then be cloned to make many pigs. Each would be a living store of spare parts such as hearts and kidneys, for transplants into people. Would this be a good thing?

• Yes, human lives would be saved. It is no different to raising pigs so they can be slaughtered for their meat.

• No, it is cruel to the pigs, and it is interfering with nature. The idea of having a pig's heart put into a human body is too dreadful to consider.

There is no worldwide agreement on whether the cloning of humans should be allowed. The laws and guidelines vary greatly from one country to another. In November 2001, the American company Advanced Cell Technology announced that it had produced the first fully cloned human embryos. Such embryos would not be grown into human beings, but would provide cells for therapeutic cloning. In the same week, the British government moved to limit greatly all work on cloning human cells, including stem cells for medical use.

Is Genetic Engineering Big Business?

Research into genetic engineering and other forms of genetics is a huge, worldwide business, and it is growing. As a comparison, think of all the money that spectators spend every year to attend all the sports events around the world. More than 1,000 times this amount is spent on genetic research every month.

Where does the money come from?

Part of the money for genetic research comes from government organizations. This includes money set aside to find gene-based answers to the major health problems of people, plants, and animals in the world. The richest nations, especially the U.S., spend the most.

Nearly all of the rest of the money comes from private sources. These vary from individual people to multinational companies. In a few cases, people with fabulous wealth donate money or set up a private project to find a genetic answer

Gaining control

"GM crops are being developed by multinational companies with the stated intention of gaining control over much of the world's food supplies."

Source: GM protest, Oneworld website, 2002

Celera Genomics of Rockville, Maryland, which helped to speed up the work of the Human Genome Organization (see panel on page 43).

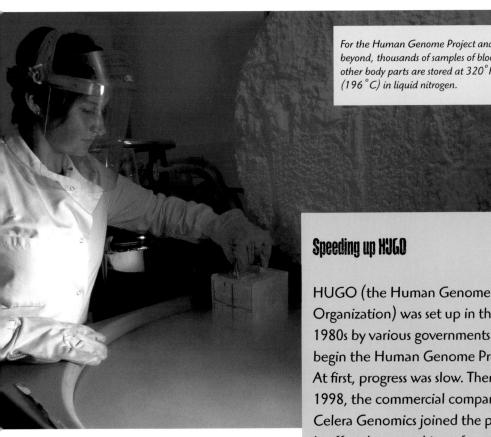

For the Human Genome Project and beyond, thousands of samples of blood and other body parts are stored at 320°F (196°C) in liquid nitrogen.

Speeding up HUGO

HUGO (the Human Genome Organization) was set up in the late 1980s by various governments to begin the Human Genome Project. At first, progress was slow. Then, in 1998, the commercial company Celera Genomics joined the project. It offered to speed it up for an early finish in 2000 instead of the estimated date of 2005. But Celera's offer was linked to the company keeping some of the information under its own control, for its own private use.

to a very specific problem. This might be a disease from which they or someone in their family suffers.

Why spend money on genetics?

In many regions, genetic engineering is being used as part of the fight against terrible diseases such as malaria, typhoid, cholera, and AIDS. Genetic engineering could also help to make drinking water clean and pure, by creating genetically engineered bugs that are harmless to us, but which kill the bugs that contaminate water. Genetic engineering could tackle the huge amount of illness and death due to the lack of food in parts of the world. It can make crops and farm animals yield more, create crops that grow in difficult conditions, and produce crops such as golden rice (see *page 28*) which contain extra vitamins.

Where are the biggest companies?

More than three-quarters of the money spent on genetics comes from private companies. As in any other business, a genetics company is set up to fill a need. If it does so, it makes a profit and continues. If not, the company goes bust. The biggest genetic engineering and biotechnology companies are based in the world's richest countries, mainly in the U.S., Europe, and Japan.

A waiting game

In January 2001, Tewolde Berhan Egziabher, head of the Environmental Protection Authority of Ethiopia, convinced many developing countries to be cautious about a headlong rush into a GM world. He argued that permission to plant GM crops should wait for more studies on safety, and also until profits could be shared more fairly. This disappointed big businesses, who had hoped to make money from selling GM crops to poorer nations.

In 2001, thread made from soy beans is exhibited in Beijing, China. A proposed patent for the genetic key to high-yield soy beans has caused fierce arguments in the country, where soy beans have been grown for thousands of years.

Why are genes patented?

People spend many years and large amounts of money inventing gadgets and machines, from cars to computers. Granting a "patent" to the inventors is seen as a fair way of rewarding them. The patent prevents others from using the invention, unless they get permission and pay money to the person who owns the patent.

Patents also apply to genes. A genetic engineering company that "invents" a useful new combination of genes, such as a tomato that lasts longer on a store shelf, is granted a patent. The patent for that combination of genes stops other people from simply copying it. If there were no patents, genetic engineering and biotechnology companies could not earn the money they need to survive.

Can you own a gene?

There are more than 750 patents around the world for major products of genetic engineering and biotechnology, such as GM crops. More than half of them are held by companies in the U.S. Europe and Japan come next. Many people in poorer countries see this as yet another example of the rich getting richer.

Patents are held not only on new combinations of genes, but on sets of genes that occur in nature, in a plant or animal. Should a person or company be able to "own" such a natural, fundamental item as the instructions for life? Suppose a rare plant is discovered in the rain forest of a poor country. Scientists from a rich country study the plant and find it has a useful gene for resisting disease. They patent the gene, put it into a GM crop, and make vast profits. Is this fair? It could be argued that the genes belong to no individual or company. They are part of nature, for everyone to share. But the scientists have done all the work, so do they deserve the reward?

Now suppose that a rare new animal is discovered in the same rain forest. It is taken in secret to a rich country and put on display by a zoo to make money. Is that the same issue? Both the plant and the animal are basically sets of genes.

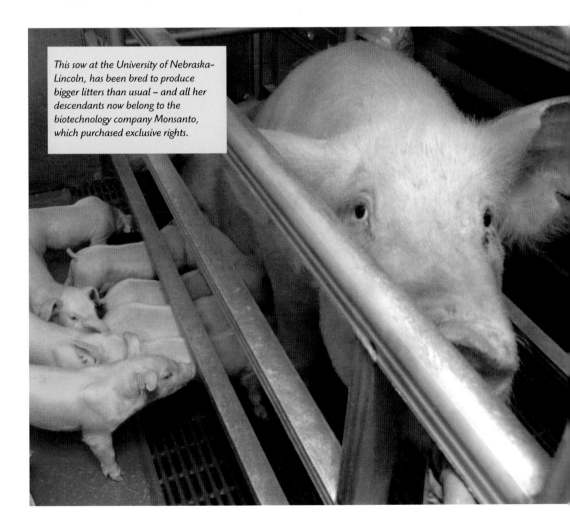

This sow at the University of Nebraska–Lincoln, has been bred to produce bigger litters than usual – and all her descendants now belong to the biotechnology company Monsanto, which purchased exclusive rights.

Should genes mean profits?

Some people argue that genes are a product, like any other. Companies chop down trees for lumber or make meat into hamburgers and sell them for profit. Genetic engineering companies should be allowed to do the same with genes. A different argument is that genes are inside every one of us and in every living thing. They are, at the very basic level, life itself. No one should be allowed to own them, charge money to use them, or make profits from them.

The pharmaceutical companies that develop and produce medicinal drugs do not simply want to help sick people. They are businesses and need to make a profit, so that they have money to develop more new drugs in the future. It takes, on average, $250 million to bring a new drug into general use.

However, there is a complicated system of limits, licenses, and regulations that prevent companies making "excessive" profits. These apply especially to medicinal drugs sold in poorer countries, which are often the places that most need the drugs but can least afford them. Perhaps similar controls should be applied to genetic engineering.

Will genetic engineering save the world?

Genetic engineering is a complex subject, and it is hard to tell how it will develop. It is also a very young science, barely 25 years old. Imagine if you could travel back in time to 1825, when the science of flowing electricity was only 25 years old. Some people at the time believed this new force was "the devil's work." Who could have predicted then how the world would one day depend on electricity?

Millions of poorer people could benefit from the "genetic revolution." But will the winners be the rich nations once again?

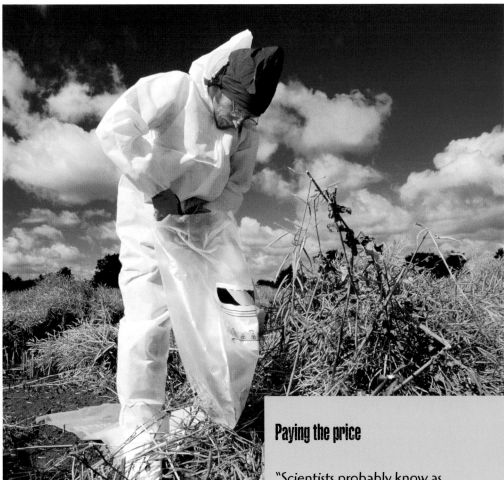

Are anti-GM protesters saving us from genetic and environmental disaster, or ruining research that could help to feed the hungry and heal the sick?

In the future, genetic engineering might feed starving millions; ease pain and suffering for millions more; and make the world a happier, healthier, safer place. Or, it might unleash nightmare diseases and superbugs, destroy vast areas of countryside, and make the rich even richer at the expense of the poor.

Evidence from other important advances in technology, such as cars, computers, and antibiotic drugs, suggests that the future may lie somewhere in between.

Paying the price

"Scientists probably know as little about the risks of genetic engineering as they did about the risks of radiation back in the 1950s. We're all aware of the price we're paying for that ignorance now – and will go on paying, probably for as long as humanity continues to exist."

Source: Mae-Wan Ho in Genetic Engineering: Dream or Nightmare? *(Gateway Books)*

It might depend not so much on the scientists and what they can do, but on society as a whole and what it wants science to achieve.

REFERENCE

GM CROPS

For comparison, one hectare is an area 100 meters by 100 meters, or one-hundredth of a square kilometer, or approximately the size of two soccer fields or 2.47 acres. The total land area of the U.S. is approximately 937 million hectares, or 2,315,000,000 acres.

AREAS OF COMMERCIAL PLANTINGS OF GM CROPS, 2000 (BY NATION)

Country	Area
USA	30.3 million hectares (up 6% from 1999; mainly GM soy bean, cotton, and canola)
Argentina	10 million hectares (up 49% from 1999, mainly GM soy bean and maize)
Canada	3 million hectares (down 25% from 1999)
China	0.5 million hectares (up 67% from 1999, mainly GM cotton)
South Africa	0.2 million hectares
Australia	0.2 million hectares
Bulgaria, France, Germany, Mexico Romania, Spain, Uruguay	Each less than 0.1 million hectares

REASONS FOR GM CROPS WORLDWIDE, 2000

Tolerance to weedkillers or herbicides	74%
Resistance to insect pests	19%
Both herbicide tolerance and insect resistance	7%

WORLDWIDE COMMERCIAL PLANTINGS OF GM CROPS, 2000 (BY CROP TYPE)

Crop	Area (percentage of total)
Soy bean	25.9 million hectares (58%)
Maize (corn)	10.3 million hectares (23%)
Cotton	5.3 million hectares (12%)
Canola	2.8 million hectares (6%)
Potato, squash, and papaya	Each less than 0.1 million hectares

GM CROP AS PROPORTION OF ALL CROPS OF THAT TYPE (GM AND NON-GM) (2000)

Crop	Proportion
Soya	36%
Cotton	16%
Canola	11%
Maize (corn)	7%

WORLDWIDE COMMERCIAL PLANTINGS OF GM CROPS

Year	Area
1995	1–2 million hectares (approximate)
1999	39.9 million hectares
2000	44.2 million hectares
2001	45–48 million hectares (approximate)

Increase in GM Crops, 1999 to 2000 (Developing Nations)

Year	Area
1999	7.1 million hectares
2000	10.7 million hectares

(Increase = up 51%)

Increase in GM Crops, 1999 to 2000 (Developed Nations)

Year	Area
1999	32.8 million hectares
2000	33.5 million hectares

(Increase = up 2%)

Source: International Service for the Acquisition of Agri-Biotech Applications (ISAAA)

GM Food Labeling

UK Laws

If a food contains GM ingredients, this must be shown on the label. But there are exceptions:

- If an ingredient obtained from a GM crop has exactly the same composition as the equivalent non-GM ingredients – e.g. refined vegetable oil – this does not need to be shown on the label.
- If small amounts (below 1%) of GM ingredients are accidentally present in non-GM ingredients, this does not need to be shown on the label.

Since 1997, foods from 11 different GM crops have been assessed for safety in the European Union. But no decisions on safety have been taken and no approvals for use have been granted or refused.

Genes and Genomes

The Human Genome

Number of genes in entire human genome: 30, 000–35, 000

Number of bases in entire human genome: 3 trillion
(printed as letters of this size, these would fill 200 telephone directories)

Participating Nations in HUGO (Human Genome Organization)

Australia, Brazil, Canada, China, Denmark, France, Germany, Israel, Italy, Japan, Korea, Mexico, Netherlands, Russia, Sweden, UK, USA (plus about 10 other nations in more minor roles)

Cost of Human Genome Organization (to June 2000)

US$250 million (£178.5 million)

Variation in Genes

Probable variation between genes of two randomly picked humans:
1 gene in 1,000 genes would be different

Probable variation between genes of randomly picked human and randomly picked chimpanzee:
1 gene in 50 genes would be different

Probable variation between genes of randomly picked human and randomly picked mouse:
1 gene in 10 genes would be different

Human Genome Timeline

1988
HUGO (Human Genome Organization) is founded by scientists from around the world.

1990
The Human Genome Project begins.

1992
The first general map shows the way in which many genes are linked.

1995
First detailed gene maps are made, for chromosomes 16 and 19.

1996
Mapping is completed for the whole set of genes activated in a human cell – in this case, a type of white blood cell.

1997
Very detailed maps are made for chromosomes 7 and X (female sex chromosome).

1998
First genome base sequence map is completed for a multi celled living thing, a worm (*Caenorhabditis elegans*).

1999
First complete map is completed for one human chromosome, number 22.

2000
Completion of first "working draft" of human genome DNA sequence.

2001
February, Initial Working Draft Sequence for DNA is published. Now the order of bases is known, figuring out how they make up genes and what the genes do are major future goals.

Genetics, Biotechnology, and Cloning Timeline

1863
Austrian Gregor Mendel's tests on peas lay foundations for science of genetics.

1900
Drosophila (fruit flies) used in early studies of genes.

1938
Hans Spemann suggests cloning by taking nucleus of one cell and inserting it into an egg cell with nucleus removed.

1940
DNA shown to be the substance that carries genes.

1953
Watson and Crick describe the double-helix structure of DNA.

1966
The genetic code is cracked, showing which codes of bases in DNA produce which products.

1967
The substance DNA ligase is isolated, which "glues" pieces of DNA together.

1970
The first artificial gene is made by gluing pieces of DNA. Restriction enzymes are used to cut and splice pieces of DNA.

1973
Improved DNA techniques produce the first recombinant DNA (gene-spliced) organism, a new variety of *E. coli* bacteria.

1976
First research begins on genetic engineering in human inherited disease. Methods of DNA sequencing discovered.

1978
Human insulin is first produced by genetic engineering. Louise Brown becomes the first "test-tube baby" (conceived outside the mother's body).

1979
Human growth hormone is made by artificial means.

1981
The first transgenic animals – genes from other animals are put into mice.

1983
Polymerase Chain Reaction (PCR) technique is used to make unlimited copies of DNA. Genetic "markers" are discovered for inherited diseases.

1984
DNA fingerprinting technique. The first genetically engineered vaccine. An entire genome is sequenced, for the AIDS virus HIV. Sheep become the first mammals cloned from embryo cells.

1985
Genetically engineered plants are tested for resistance to insects, viruses, and bacteria.

1986
The first field tests for genetically engineered plants – tobacco.

1988
The first American patent for a genetically altered animal.

1990
Artificially produced chymosin for cheese making is the first product of genetic engineering approved for the human food industry in the U.S..
Gene therapy treatment is performed successfully on a four-year-old girl.
A genetically altered cow produces human milk proteins for human babies.

1993
The first cloned human cells, taken from embryos.

1994
The Flavr-Savr tomato is the first genetically engineered whole food approved for sale in the U.S.. The first breast cancer gene is discovered. Calves are cloned from cells of early embryos.

1996
The gene associated with Parkinson's disease is discovered.
Dolly the sheep, first mammal cloned from the specialized cell of an adult.

1997
The first herbicide- and insect-resistant crops introduced on a large scale.

1998
Experiments with cell-repair genes show human life may be extended 40%.

2000
A cloned cow shows that cloning can rejuvenate cells. Biotechnology study focuses on human aging problems.

2001
President George W. Bush supports research on stem cells. Britain moves to restrict greatly work on human cloning.

2002
Genetically altered and cloned pigs suggest this research could provide spare-part organs for human transplants. Dolly the sheep has arthritis, which would normally occur in a much older sheep – is she as old as herself and her clone added together? The American company ACT announces the growing of cloned human embryos to six-cell stage, solely for therapeutic uses (medical treatments).

GLOSSARY

allergy When a substance such as dust or pollen, which is normally harmless, causes reactions such as coughing, sneezing, wheezing, skin rash, or digestive upset.

artificial selection When people choose which individuals from a type of animal or plant breed together, rather than letting nature take its course.

bases Chemical units that are part of the genetic substance DNA. They carry information as chemical codes.

biodiversity Variation in types of animals, plants, and other living things.

cell Tiny unit or "building block" of life. Most cells are so small that 50 placed end to end stretch only 1 mm. The human body contains billions of cells.

chromosome A very long piece of the genetic material DNA, which is coiled and supercoiled to produce an X-shaped object just about visible under a microscope.

clones Genetic copies – living things with exactly the same genes as each other.

DNA Deoxyribonucleic acid, the chemical substance that carries the genetic information (genes) for how living things grow, develop, and survive.

domesticated Altered and "tamed" for human use, such as a pet or farm crop.

dominant Describing a gene that exerts its effect, despite the presence of a similar partner gene, which is less powerful or "recessive."

egg An egg cell contains a full set of genes from the mother, ready to join with a sperm cell from the father, to produce a fertilized egg, which grows into a new individual.

embryo A very early stage in the development of an individual, after the fertilized egg has begun to divide. An embryo contains anything from a couple of cells to thousands.

field trial When plants are test-grown in small areas in fields, before they go on to large-scale commercial growing.

fingerprinting Genetic fingerprinting finds unique features of a sample of DNA, which show that it almost certainly came from a specific individual.

gene therapy Treatment for a disorder by changing or altering the genes of a living thing, rather than treating its body or chemical processes.

genes The instructions or information for a living thing, so that it can grow, develop, and survive. They are in the form of the chemical substance DNA.

genetic condition A medical problem or disorder that is due to a fault in the genes rather than other causes such as physical injury or infection by germs.

genetic counselor A medical expert on genes, genetic disorders, and how they are passed from parents to offspring.

genetic engineering Altering, changing or manipulating genes, for example by moving them from one kind of living thing to another.

genetic modification Modifying or altering genes – see *genetic engineering*.

genome The whole set of genes for an individual living thing.

helix A shape like a corkscrew.

heredity The study of how genes and bodily features are passed from parents to offspring, over many generations.

hormones Chemical substances in a living thing that control processes such as growth or sexual development.

inherited Passed from parents to offspring.

markers Substances that are next to or near a certain gene in the DNA, and which can be easily shown up and identified by laboratory tests.

mutation Change in a gene. Mutations may be "good," with positive effects on survival; "bad" with negative effects; or neutral with no effect.

phage Short for bacteriophage, a type of virus (tiny living thing) that attacks the microbes known as bacteria.

pollen Tiny, dustlike particles or grains containing the plant's male cells, produced by the male parts of a flower.

proteins Chemical substances that form the living framework of a body, building muscles, bones, and other parts.

recessive Describing a gene that cannot exert its effects because it is "overpowered" by a similar partner gene, which is "dominant."

recombinant A combination of genes that does not occur naturally or which has been put together artificially.

restriction enzymes Chemicals that cut or split long pieces of DNA at certain places, into shorter pieces or fragments.

RNA Ribonucleic acid, a chemical substance involved in building proteins and other substances in the body in accordance with the genetic instructions in DNA.

selective breeding See *artificial selection*.

sperm See *egg cell*.

stem cells Cells from the early stage of development in a living thing (embryo), which have not yet become specialized, but have the ability to do so.

therapeutic cloning Making clones (genetic identical copies) for the purpose of treating illness and curing disease.

toxin Harmful or poisonous substance.

transgenic A living thing that has genes from other types of living things added to it.

vaccine A substance that causes the body to become resistant, or immune, to germs which cause disease, without actually causing the disease.

virus A part-living thing, far smaller than an ordinary microbe such as bacteria. It must take over living cells and destroy them in order to function and multiply.

FURTHER INFORMATION

BOOKS

Cloning: Frontiers of Genetic Engineering by David Jefferis (Megatech, 1999)
A survey of genetics as a science, exploring the cell as the unit of life, human genomes, the cloning of animals and perhaps humans; also organ transplants, gene therapy, genetic farming, and "controlled evolution."

Genetic Engineering by James D. Torr (Greenhaven, 2000)
A longer and more detailed treatment of the issues involved in genes, genetic modification, and the potential for this area of science to change our world.

Genetic Engineering: Debating the Benefits and Concerns by Karen Judson (Lerner, 2001)
Issues connected with animal and human cloning are combined with basic principles of genetics, gene therapy, gene tests, and discrimination based on genetics.

Genetic Engineering: Progress or Peril? by Linda Tagliaferro (Lerner, 1997)
The basics of genetic engineering, its potential, hopes, and the challenges it faces – ethical, moral, and legal – in the twenty-first century.

Genetics (Science Fact Files) by Richard Beatty (Hodder Wayland, 2001)
A straightforward examination of genetics topics with essential information, clearly designed.

Superhumans: A Beginner's Guide to Bionics by Simon Beecroft (Copper Beech, 1998)
A brief look at the history and a longer gaze into the future, and what might happen as plants, animals, and humans are engineered physically, chemically, mechanically, and genetically.

The Complete Idiot's Guide to Decoding Your Genes by Linda Tagliaferro, Mark Vincent Bloom (Alpha Books, 1999)
Everyday language explains the role genes play in shaping who we are; genetic engineering of plants, animals, and people; cloning; DNA in the courts; genetic testing.

The Monster Garden by Vivien Alcock (Houghton Mifflin Co, 2000)
Many aspects of genetics disguised in a fantasy tale about a girl, Frankie, whose scientist dad works in a top-secret laboratory, and whose older brother steals some mysterious goo from there.

OTHER TITLES

Genetics and Genetic Engineering editor Lisa Yount (Greenhaven, 1997)

Biomedical Ethics: Opposing Viewpoints editor Tamara L. Roleff (Greenhaven, 1998)

Genetic Engineering by Jenny Bryan (Hodder Wayland, 1997)

Genetics: The Impact on Our Lives by Paul Dowswell (Hodder Wayland, 2001)

MAGAZINES

New Scientist Weekly British science magazine suitable for many non-science readers, which takes special notice of newsworthy or controversial matters in the fields of genetics, genetic engineering, and cloning.

Scientific American Monthly American magazine known for its clear diagrams, which regularly includes features on all aspects of genetics.

Popular Science and *Discover* American science magazines that often feature genetics and genetic engineering.

ORGANIZATIONS & WEBSITES

**www.oneworld.org/penguin/genetics/
  home.html**
Tiki's guide to Genetic Engineering gives introductory facts for young people, with guides for action and links to other sites, like the U.S. Biodemocracy Campaign.

www.sanger.ac.uk
**The Wellcome Trust Sanger Institute
Hinxton, Cambridge, CB10 1SA, UK**
The Wellcome Trust Sanger Institute is one of the leading gene research centers in the world and plays a central role in the Human Genome Project.

www.ornl.gov/hgmis
U.S. Dept of energy site with a vast array of links, explaining almost everything you could wish to know about the Human Genome Project, research, social and ethical issues.

www.greenpeace.org
Greenpeace USA offers, press releases, supermarket campaigns, and general information about genetic engineering.

www.safe-food.org
U.S. Mothers for Natural Law offer information about genetic engineering, the issues and dangers, and campaigns for safety in food.

www.hfea.gov.uk
Britain's Human Fertilization and Embryology Authority is the official body that regulates, licenses and collects information on fertility treatments, as well as human embryo research, cloning, and various other fertility matters.

www.asgt.org
The American Society of Gene Therapy informs the media and public about new developments in gene therapy and gene therapy research, including appropriate reporting on the effects of gene therapy on patients.

**The Council for Responsible Genetics
5 Upland Rd, Suite 3, Cambridge,
MA 02140**
www.gene-watch.org
This U.S. organization of scientists is helping to keep the public informed about issues in genetics.

INDEX

golden rice 28, 43
governments 41, 42, 43
growth hormone 22

heart disease 15
hemophilia 23
hepatitis 23
HIV 25
hormones 23
human clones 40
Human Genome Project 7, 42, 43

identical twins 14, 36, 38, 40
infection 30
inherited conditions 14, 15, 16
insulin 23
interferon 24

Japan 43, 45

Kac, Eduardo 10

lungs 18, 19

maize (corn) 5, 28, 29, 31, 32, 33, 35
malaria 43
medicinal drugs 24, 25, 38, 46
Mexico 33
mice 18
microbes 21, 22, 24, 28
milk 25, 26, 38, 39
mucus 18, 19
multiple gene conditions 15
muscular dystrophy 18
mutation 5, 13, 39

nicotine 31

oil 25

oilseed rape 24, 25, 34
oranges 26, 31
organic farming 33
oxygen 13

parents 14, 15, 16, 27, 36
patents 20, 44, 45
phages 10, 11
pharmaceutical companies 46
plants 5, 7, 24, 25, 26, 29, 30, 32, 34, 36, 38, 45
poisons 30
pollen grains 33
polymerase chain reaction (PCR) 21
potatoes 26, 31
profits 43, 44, 46
proteins 9
protesters 30, 47

rabbits 10, 38
radioactivity 13
rain forest 45
recessive genes 14
research funding 42
resistance 30, 39
restriction enzymes 10
ribonucleic acid (RNA) 9
rice 26, 28, 43
ripening genes 29

salmon farming 27
Scotland 37
selective breeding 21, 26, 27, 31
sewage pollution 25
shellfish 24
sickle-cell anemia 13, 15
skin 14
South America 5
soy beans 5, 28, 29, 31, 44
sperm 14, 17
spina bifida 17
stem cells 19, 40, 41

sunflowers 25
supermarkets 31

technology 20
termination of pregnancy 17
therapeutic cloning 40, 41
tissues 17
tobacco 31
tomatoes 29, 44
toxins 30
transgenic life forms 11
transplants 40, 41
trials 30, 32
tuberous sclerosis 14
twins 14, 36, 38, 40
typhoid 43

UK 34
US Supreme Court 20
USA 5, 7, 29, 41, 42, 43, 45

vaccines 25
viruses 10, 18, 24, 25, 28, 34
vitamins 28, 43

waste disposal 25
Watson, James 9
weedkiller resistance 28, 34
wheat 5, 26, 29, 32
wine brewing 20, 21
womb 38, 40

yeasts 20, 21